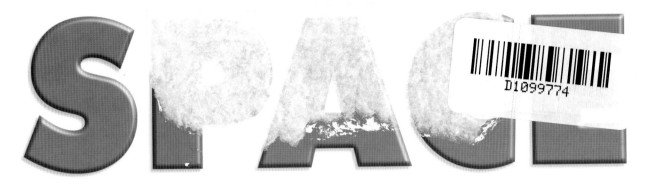

# KNOW HOW KNOW WHY

# SPACE

Written by Martin Mobberley

Illustrations by Stephen Sweet

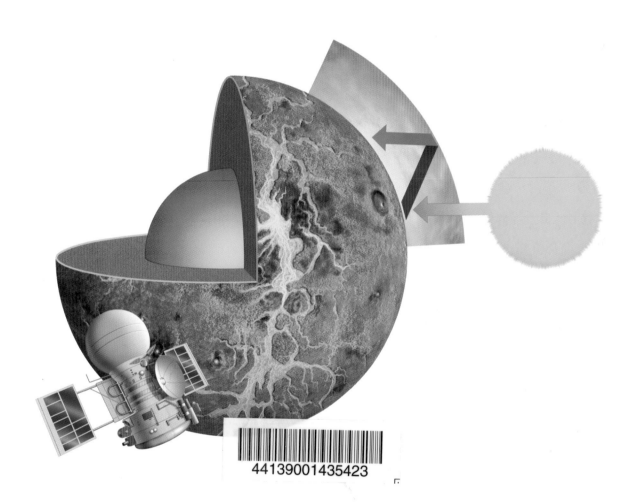

Licensed exclusively to Top That Publishing Ltd
Tide Mill Way, Woodbridge, Suffolk, IP12 1AP, UK
www.topthatpublishing.com
Copyright © 2014 Tide Mill Media
All rights reserved
0 2 4 6 8 9 7 5 3 1
Printed and bound in China

# THE UNIVERSE

A vast, perhaps infinite, mass of galaxies, older than we can possibly imagine, the universe is measured in 'light years' due to its phenomenal size. Whether it was formed by a 'big bang', or set to collapse in a 'big crunch', scientists have created their own theories about the secrets that it may hold...

## How big is the universe

The universe is so big that astronomers use the distance that light travels in one year to measure the parts of it we can see. A beam of light, or a radio wave, travels 300,000 km in one second. In just over one second, light can travel from Earth to the Moon. In eight minutes a beam of sunlight can travel from the Sun to Earth, so the Sun is eight light-minutes away.

*8 minutes*

## What was the 'big bang'

Most astronomers think that around fourteen billion years ago, the universe suddenly came into existence and increased rapidly in size. There was nothing there before the 'big bang' – no stars, no galaxies, no space and, wait for it... no time. So there was nothing before the 'big bang', because it created time! The universe is still expanding, although the gravitational pull of all the galaxies has slowed the expansion down.

*An artist's impression of the 'big bang'.*

## How far can astronomers see into the universe

With powerful telescopes, astronomers can see galaxies that are over ten billion light years away. The light from them has taken ten billion years to get to us! More than ten billion light years is almost the same distance as a hundred billion trillion kilometres, that's 100,000,000,000,000,000,000,000 km! That's a very long way! However, we cannot say that the universe definitely 'stops' somewhere. We can only judge from what we can see in light years which is galaxies of more than ten billion light years away. We reach a horizon where we can see no more – which means that the universe could go on forever!

*A space observatory.*

*The Hubble Space Telescope allows astronomers to see distant galaxies.*

*The 'universe' is the name given to everything out there and it could be infinite*

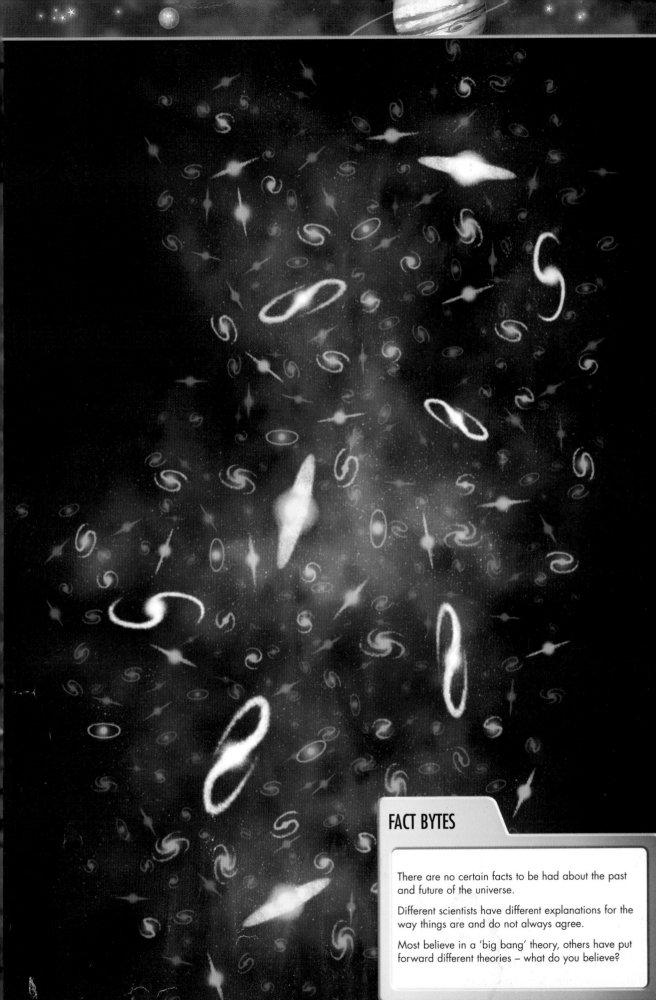

## FACT BYTES

There are no certain facts to be had about the past and future of the universe.

Different scientists have different explanations for the way things are and do not always agree.

Most believe in a 'big bang' theory, others have put forward different theories – what do you believe?

# THE SUN

The Sun makes life on our planet possible by giving us great amounts of light and heat. It is situated at the centre of our solar system and all the planets and other objects orbit around it. Without the Sun, no living thing would be able to survive and our planet would be completely frozen.

## Where did the Sun come from

The Sun is made up mainly of hydrogen gas, which is the most common element in the universe. When the universe was much younger than it is today, the part of space where our solar system is now would have been full of hydrogen gas and dust. Over billions of years, this gas and dust would slowly have moved together, due to gravity, and a large amount of hydrogen gas would have concentrated in the middle. As the sheer mass at the centre became more concentrated there would have come a point when nuclear reactions began to take place and the gas started to shine! It probably took place about five billion (5,000,000,000) years ago.

## Why do we have seasons

We have seasons – spring, summer, autumn and winter – because Earth is tilted. This tilting causes different parts of the globe to be positioned towards the Sun at different times of the year. If the northern hemisphere is tilted towards the Sun, it will be summer there. At the same time, the southern hemisphere will be tilted away from the Sun and it will be winter. Autumn and spring occur when Earth is tilted neither towards nor away from the Sun. This means different sides of the world experience opposite seasons at the same time.

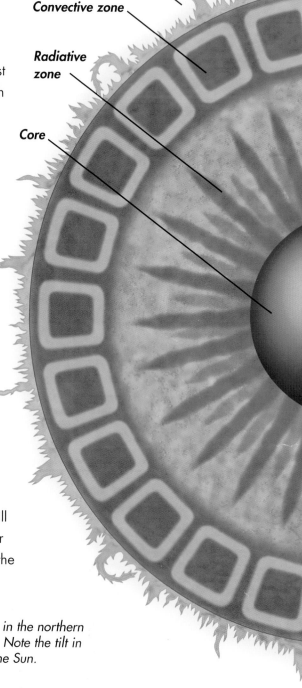

Corona
Convective zone
Radiative zone
Core

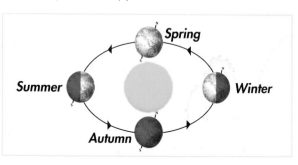

Spring
Summer
Winter
Autumn

*The seasons in the northern hemisphere. Note the tilt in relation to the Sun.*

**WARNING!** The Sun is very d
directly at it or look

## How hot is the Sun

The centre of the Sun is an extreme 15 million°C – so hot that planets millions of kilometres away receive its heat! The Sun's temperature decreases towards its surface where it is about 6,000°C. This is cool for the Sun, but it is actually about 16 times hotter than boiling water! At the outermost layer, the temperature rises again to well over 1 million°C! During the first half of the twentieth century, Sir Arthur Eddington explained that heat and light is generated by the Sun when particles called protons crash into the Sun's core.

*Sir Arthur Eddington.*

## What is a sunspot

A sunspot is a darker and cooler region on the Sun's surface caused by intense magnetic activity. The Sun's surface temperature is around 6,000°C, but the centre of the sunspot will only be around 4,000°C.
The Sun has a diameter more than a hundred times that of Earth and big sunspots are bigger than Earth too!

### FACT BYTES

The corona is the outermost layer of the Sun. It stretches millions of kilometres into space.

The centre of the Sun is made of helium.

The Sun spins around once every 27.4 days.

s. You should NEVER stare a telescope at it.

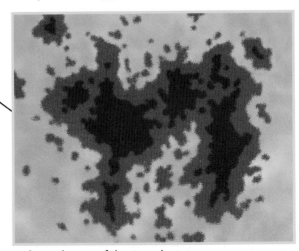

*Enlarged area of the Sun depicting a sunspot.*

# MERCURY

Mercury is the second-smallest planet in our solar system. It's also the closest to the Sun. It has the widest range in temperatures of any planet, from a chilly –180°C at night to a scorching 430°C during the day. If you were standing on Mercury, the Sun would look three times larger than it does from Earth.

## How big is Mercury

The respective sizes of Earth (left) and Mercury (right).

Mercury has a diameter of 4,880 km, and is one-third the size of Earth. It is the smallest of the eight planets in our solar system.

## How hot is Mercury

Although Mercury is the planet closest to the Sun, Venus is slightly hotter because it has an atmosphere that traps the heat. Mercury has no atmosphere, but has the most extreme range of temperatures. They range from 430°C in sunlight to –180°C at night.

**430°C**

**–180°C**

Mercury experiences extreme temperature variation.

### FACT BYTES

A Mercury year is 88 Earth days long!

Mercury is roughly the same age as the Sun – 4.5 billion years old!

The Mariner 10 space probe.

## How many times has it been visited

Two space probes have visited Mercury. The Mariner 10 was launched in 1973 and flew past Mercury in 1974. The MESSENGER was launched in 2004, with the first of three flybys occurring in 2008.

**Rocky crust**

**Molten core**

**Silicate rock**

## Why does Mercury stay in orbit ?

Mercury is very close to the Sun, but there is no danger of it falling into the Sun. Gravity forces all the planets to rotate 'around' the Sun: they would only fall in if they were stopped from going round. As there is no air in space, there is nothing to slow the planets down in their orbits.

## How long is Mercury's year ?

One year on Mercury is equal to 88 Earth days. However, a day on Mercury is almost twice as long as a year! This causes the Sun to crawl very slowly across the sky. If you were to stand on the surface of Mercury, the time from one sunrise to another would be equal to 176 Earth days. These long days and nights cause temperatures to rise very high and fall very low.

## When do the orbits of the Sun and Mercury cross ?

This happens about thirteen or fourteen times each century. The last time was on 8th November, 2006 and the next time will be on 9th May, 2016. Only astronomers with the right equipment can photograph these events as the Sun is dangerously bright and will blind or seriously affect the sight of anyone who looks at it through a telescope.

*The Mercury landscape.*

**MERCURY**

# VENUS

**Gustav Holst called Venus the 'Bringer of Peace' in his famous 'Planets' suite. With its bright white clouds, visible in the night sky, it is aptly named. Should we get closer, however, we'd see that under those clouds exists a cratered surface on which nothing could survive, smothered under its boiling hot atmosphere.**

*An artist's impression of Venus as seen from Earth.*

## Why is Venus so bright ?

It is partly due to its covering of white clouds, which reflect 60 per cent of the Sun's rays back into space. We measure how easy things are to see on a 'magnitude' scale. Venus can reach magnitude −4 – making it one of the brightest objects in the night sky.

## Has a spacecraft landed on Venus ?

Spacecraft have landed and orbited Venus since the 1970s. One of the first to land was Russian spacecraft, *Venera 9*, in 1975. It collected data and sent back pictures of Venus.

## How close is Venus to Earth ?

Venus and Mars both get very near to Earth – relatively speaking! Mars can come within 56 million kilometres of Earth and did so in August 2003. Venus gets even closer, at 39 million kilometres from Earth, but is then between Earth and the Sun so cannot be seen.

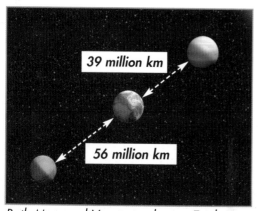

*Both Mars and Venus get close to Earth.*

39 million km

56 million km

Rocky crust

Semi-solid core of iron and nickel

Rocky mantle

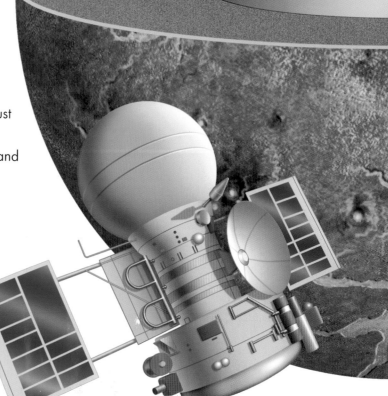

*The Russian Venera 9 that landed on Venus.*

## How hot is it on Venus ?

Venus is three-quarters the distance of Earth from the Sun. If we didn't know better, we might expect it to be a planet where life could exist near the cooler polar regions. However, the surface temperature can reach 470°C. This is because the thick clouds and atmosphere, which is mainly carbon dioxide, makes Venus just like a huge greenhouse, trapping the Sun's heat.

## What is it like on Venus' surface ?

The dusty and bumpy surface of Venus is littered with impact craters and volcanoes. Thick clouds of sulphur dioxide, capable of producing lightning much like the clouds on Earth, permanently fill the skies. The planet's rolling plains are covered in gloomy darkness, caused by the dense clouds that obscure the surface and reflect about 60 per cent of the sunlight that falls on them back into space.

### FACT BYTES

Venus probably once had large amounts of water like Earth but it all boiled away. If Earth had been any closer to the Sun, it may have suffered the same terrible fate as Venus.

*The surface of Venus could be volcanic.*

# EARTH AND MOON

Our planet is unique, with an atmosphere made of gases existing in perfect harmony to sustain the life underneath. We walk around on the thin crust, suspended on a moving, molten and plastic-like layer called the mantle. Despite having just one moon, even Earth's tides are affected by its presence.

## Why is our Moon so large ?

*Our Moon is relatively large, its diameter being more than a quarter of Earth's.*

Our Moon is 3,470 km in diameter, more than a quarter the diameter of Earth. There are larger moons in the solar system, but they all belong to the giant planets. Astronomers believe that billions of years ago, another planet passed through the inner solar system and bumped into Earth, moving loads of molten rock into space. This rock eventually reformed as the Moon. The oldest rocks on the surface of the Moon are estimated to be 4.6 billion years old.

## What shape is Earth ?

*A pumpkin shape?*

Our planet is not the perfect sphere that you might imagine – it is actually a bit larger around the middle! This makes it slightly pumpkin-shaped. A recent study showed that this bulge was actually on the increase, due to glacial melting at the poles which has led to more water building up around the equatorial area.

## What is so special about Earth ?

At about 149 million kilometres from the Sun, Earth is at exactly the right distance away for things to survive. In addition, Earth's gravity is not too small (it's 12,700 km in diameter) so the atmosphere doesn't escape, but it's not too big, so lighter, poisonous gases are not retained. Earth also has plenty of water which is essential for life.

*Life on Earth's landscape is uniquely sustained.*

*e remains
n with
lanet?*

## Why does the Moon appear to change shape

The Moon orbits Earth every four weeks, so that there are just over 29 days between full moons. When the Moon is directly behind Earth, the Sun is shining straight onto the side we see, so it looks full.
When the Moon is at right angles to the Sun–Earth line it looks half full. When the Moon is close to the Sun in our sky, the other side of the Moon is being illuminated and we just see a crescent. We always see the same side of the Moon, though, because it also rotates on its axis in four weeks.

*The waning patterns of the Moon.*

## What is an eclipse

When two things in the sky cross paths, one of the objects will block the light of the other. When the Moon comes between the Sun and Earth, the light reaching us will be affected. This is a 'solar' eclipse. If they cross slightly, then we call it a 'partial' solar eclipse. If our light is totally blocked, it is known as a 'total' eclipse and everything goes dark! You need to be in exactly the right place in the world to experience this. The Sun and the Moon will appear to be the same size and 'fit' over each other. When Earth passes between the Sun and the Moon, it is known as a lunar eclipse. The Moon will turn a dark red, as the light passing through our atmosphere is 'bent' onto the Moon.

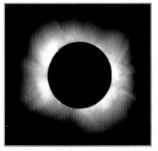

*A total eclipse.*

### FACT BYTES

The amazing combination of gases which make up our atmosphere is 78% nitrogen, 21% oxygen and 1% of other gases.

Humans haven't existed for very long at all – primitive human life began here about 200,000 years ago, but the oldest rocks discovered so far in the Earth's crust are 3,900 million or so years old!

**EARTH AND MOON**

# MARS

Mars is the fourth planet from the Sun in the solar system. Its mysterious red surface, littered with impact craters, mountains, canyons and volcanoes has captivated astronomers for hundreds of years. It is home to the highest mountain and the deepest canyon in the solar system.

## How long is a 'Mars year'

Mars rotates on its axis just like Earth, but it takes a little longer than Earth which means one Mars day lasts 24 hours and 37 minutes. Mars also goes around the Sun just like Earth, but it takes Mars nearly two Earth years to complete its orbit. This means that a Martian year is 667 days long – nearly twice as long as an Earth year! Mars is about 230 million kilometres away from the Sun and has a diameter of only 6,790 km.

## Could life exist on Mars

For over 100 years it was thought that the temperature on Mars, although much colder than on Earth, might sustain life, much as life can exist in the Arctic and Antarctic on Earth. However, when the first space probes flew past Mars in 1965, it showed craters like those on our Moon and measured that the atmosphere was 100 times thinner than Earth's. Since then, however, scientists have found strong evidence to suggest that water once flowed on the surface of Mars and simple life may once have existed there.

## Why is Mars red ?

Mars is red because its soil is rich in iron oxide. Some astronomers think that at least some of the planet's iron came from meteorites – a theory supported by the fact that Mars' surface is covered with impact craters. The 'blood-like' colour is one reason why it is named after the Roman god of war.

*Space probes have not found any signs of life on Mars.*

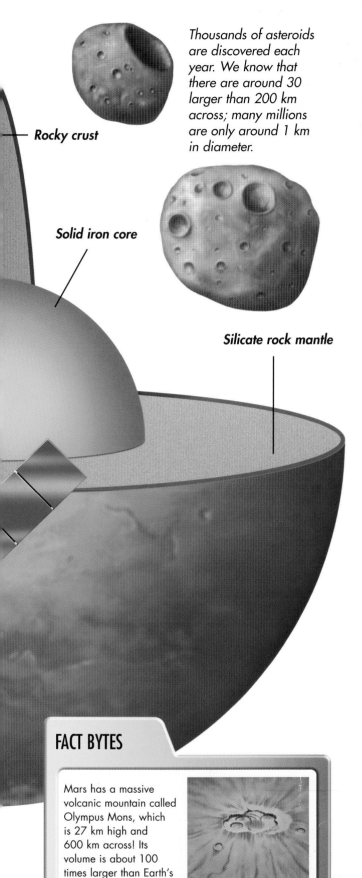

— Rocky crust

Thousands of asteroids are discovered each year. We know that there are around 30 larger than 200 km across; many millions are only around 1 km in diameter.

Solid iron core

Silicate rock mantle

## What is a 'captured' asteroid

There are hundreds of thousands of asteroids in the asteroid belt between Mars and Jupiter. Mars has two tiny moons, called Phobos and Deimos, which are asteroids that have been 'drawn in' or 'captured' by Mars' gravity.

## What are 'Martian canals'

In the late 1800s and early 1900s, various astronomers reported seeing straight lines on the Martian surface, when viewed through telescopes. The most famous of these astronomers was Percival Lowell who built a huge telescope in Arizona to study Mars. In an age when people were inspired by voyage and discovery, emphasised by the popularity of Jules Verne's book *Journey to the Centre of the Earth,* many people were convinced by his findings. However, by the end of the twentieth century, it was obvious that Mars might only be able to support primitive life. The canals had been a trick of the eye and the blurring effect of Earth's atmosphere.

### FACT BYTES

Mars has a massive volcanic mountain called Olympus Mons, which is 27 km high and 600 km across! Its volume is about 100 times larger than Earth's largest volcano.

*Mars' surface appears red to us because it contains iron oxide dust. The 'blood-like' colour is one reason why it is named after the Roman god of war.*

# JUPITER

A true giant, Jupiter has many interesting features, including its famous 'Great Red Spot'. With incredible gravitational and magnetic fields, it is the largest planet in the solar system, and the fifth furthest away from the Sun.

## How big is Jupiter ?

Jupiter is huge. It has an equatorial diameter of 142,000 km, that's eleven times wider than Earth. In fact, you could fit 1,300 Earths inside Jupiter with room to spare! Despite Jupiter's size, it spins on its axis in just under ten hours.

## How far is Jupiter from the Sun ?

Jupiter is about 780 million kilometres from the Sun – around five times further away than Earth. Light, travelling at 300,000 km per second, takes over 40 minutes to get to Jupiter. As it is so far away, it takes nearly twelve Earth years to orbit the Sun. The distance between Jupiter and its nearest neighbour, Saturn, is also massive. Saturn is twice as far from Earth as Jupiter is! There are 617 million kilometres between them.

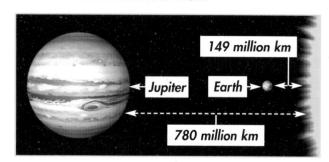

149 million km

Jupiter   Earth

780 million km

## Why has it got so many moons ?

Jupiter has over sixty natural satellites, or moons. It has so many because it is so massive and over billions of years has captured more and more objects in its huge gravitational field. The four largest moons, known as the 'Galilean moons', are called Io, Europa, Ganymede and Callisto, and are similar in size to our own Moon. These four moons can be spotted as faint stars through a small pair of binoculars. Jupiter's gravity pulled the comet Shoemaker-Levy 9 into the giant planet in July 1994. Jupiter was covered in 'bruises' from the impact for months afterwards.

Atmosphere of hydrogen and helium

Outer mantle

Inner mantle

Rocky core

Europa
Diameter 3,138 km

## How strong is Jupiter's magnetism ?

Jupiter has the strongest magnetic field of any planet in the solar system. The field is 40 times stronger than that of Earth and is generated deep within the planet by electric currents in a strange liquid called metallic hydrogen. This also gives rise to powerful radio emissions.

## Why can't we land on Jupiter ?

Jupiter does not have a surface as such. The features we see are all part of its upper atmosphere. If you sent a spacecraft to Jupiter it would just descend through more and more dense layers of hydrogen gas, which eventually become metallic hydrogen liquid. Somewhere very deep inside there is probably a rocky core.

## What is the Great Red Spot ?

The Great Red Spot is a gigantic rotating storm, bigger than the whole of Earth, which is found in Jupiter's southern hemisphere. The storm is so large that it has survived for at least 170 years and maybe for over 300 years. It can easily be seen using a small telescope.

*Great Red Spot*

**JUPITER**

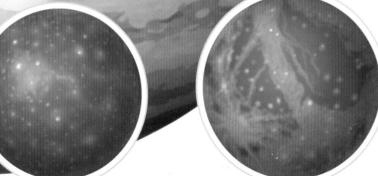

| Callisto | Ganymede | Io |
| Diameter 4,800 km | Diameter 5,262 km | Diameter 3,630 km |

# SATURN

With its massive spinning ring system, consisting mostly of ice particles with a smaller amount of rocky debris and dust, Saturn is one of the most beautiful objects in the night sky. The planet itself is nearly all gas – probably with a rocky core. A little smaller than Jupiter, it is the sixth planet from our Sun and the second-largest in our solar system.

## Why has Saturn got rings **?**

*Did an icy moon break up to form Saturn's rings?*

Many astronomers think that Saturn's rings may be the result of an icy moon that came too close to Saturn and broke up. Saturn is not the only planet to have a system of rings. The other giant planets, Jupiter, Uranus and Neptune, have extremely feeble ring systems, which are too faint to be seen from Earth. Saturn's spectacular rings make it the most beautiful object to see through a telescope.

*Liquid metallic hydrogen.*

*Outer core.*

*Inner rocky core.*

## How big are Saturn's rings **?**

Saturn's rings span a distance of over 300,000 km, with an average thickness of around 1 km. They are made up of millions of icy particles, with some combinations of dust and other chemicals. The particles range in size from a grain of sugar to the size of a house! The rings can be viewed from Earth using a modern telescope.

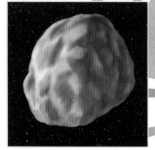

*The rings are made from icy chunks such as this.*

### FACT BYTES

Saturn spins so fast that forces cause the equator to bulge outwards – it looks a little like a squashed football!

Astronomers have discovered daytime clouds on Titan and believe it may have an atmosphere – which means it might be able to support life.

*Jupiter has a diameter of 142,000 km*

_At 5,150 km in diameter, Titan is Saturn's largest moon._

_Spinning rings._

_An atmosphere of hydrogen and helium._

## What is Saturn's largest moon

Although Saturn has no moons as easy to see as Jupiter's four big moons, it does have a moon called Titan, which is over 5,000 km in diameter. It orbits Saturn around once every sixteen days. It is easy to spot with a big pair of binoculars or a telescope.

## Why is there a big gap between the rings

Astronomers knew little about the gaps in the rings before space probes visited the planet. The largest of these gaps is called the Cassini division and is nearly 5,000 km wide. The gaps are formed by the gravitational pull of Saturn's moons on the millions of icy chunks making up the rings. The gravitational force of the moon Mimas causes the Cassini gap.

## Can I see the rings with a telescope

If a telescope is on a tripod and Saturn's rings are wide open, a magnification of less than twenty times will reveal the rings, but 100 times will show them very clearly. To the naked eye Saturn looks just like a bright star.

## How large is Saturn

Saturn has an equatorial diameter of over 120,000 km, so it is a bit smaller than Jupiter. However, the visible rings span 300,000 km from tip to tip, which is nearly twice the diameter of Jupiter. Unfortunately, Saturn is a very long way from the Sun – over 1,300 million kilometres. This is almost twice as far as Jupiter and so it appears much smaller. As it is so far away it takes over 29 years to orbit the Sun.

_aturn has a diameter of 20,000 km_

SATURN

# URANUS

With its lovely blue-green appearance, Uranus must have been an exciting discovery for astronomers. Its distinctive features include a strange rotation system and many moons, all of which are named after characters found in the writings of Alexander Pope and William Shakespeare. It has a narrow ring system, but unlike those of Saturn which are pale in colour, they are dark, as they are made from dark-coloured dust particles.

## How was Uranus discovered ?

*Herschel discovered Uranus from his garden!*

Uranus was discovered on 13th March, 1781 by William Herschel, using a hand-made telescope in the back garden of his house in Bath, England. The house has now been made into a museum. Herschel thought Uranus was a comet when he first saw it. In 1787, he discovered two of Uranus' moons – Titania and Oberon.

*You couldn't breathe on Uranus as methane makes the atmosphere poisonous.*

## What makes Uranus unique ?

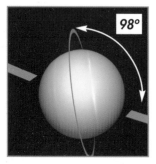

98°

Uranus is the only planet in the solar system to spin on its side. It spins in the same direction as it travels, rolling around its orbit. No one knows for certain what happened to Uranus to make it like this. However, some astronomers believe some kind of collision, billions of years ago, may have caused Uranus' 98 degree tilt.

*Uranus' tilt means it also has a strong magnetic field.*

Ariel
Diameter 1,160 km

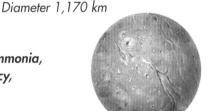

Umbriel
Diameter 1,170 km

Titania
Diameter 1,580 km

**Mantle with ammonia, methane and icy, gaseous water**

**Rocky core**

**Atmosphere of hydrogen, helium and methane**

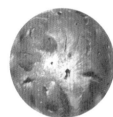

Oberon
Diameter 1,550 km

## How many moons orbit Uranus ?

Uranus has over twenty moons. The four largest ones are called Ariel, Umbriel, Titania and Oberon. Another moon, called Miranda, is less than 500 km in diameter and has a strange grooved and cratered surface, unlike any other moons in the solar system. This could have been caused by another moon crashing into it.

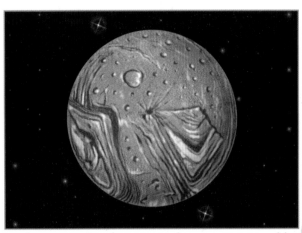

With its carved surface, Miranda is unique. It could have been shattered by another moon crashing into it, reforming with a crazy jagged surface.

## How can Uranus be spotted ?

In theory, Uranus can be seen as a faint star with the naked eye from a very dark site. You need a pair of binoculars or a small telescope to see it easily. With a large telescope, it appears as a greenish disc. It can be seen all year round in the constellation of Aquarius and is best seen in August.

## How far away is the Sun ?

Uranus is about 2,900 million kilometres from the Sun. That's twice as far away as Saturn! Light from the Sun takes nearly three hours to reach Uranus. At over 50,000 km in diameter, Uranus is a giant planet, but it is still less than half the diameter of Saturn.

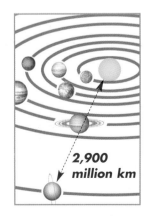

2,900 million km

### FACT BYTES

Uranus is the third largest planet in the solar system.

The reason Uranus is blue-green is because the methane gas in the atmosphere absorbs red light.

**URANUS**

**Neptune is the fourth-largest planet in the solar system and the furthest from the Sun. It is home to the fastest winds in the solar system, which power across this vivid blue planet at speeds of over 2,000 km/h. It has thirteen moons and a spectacular system of rings.**

*Atmosphere of hydrogen, helium and methane gase*

## How was Neptune discovered ?

*Astronomers Galle and D'Arrest.*

Neptune has the honour of being the first planet to be predicted on paper before it was actually seen. In 1845–1846, French mathematician, Urbain Le Verrier, predicted the existence of the planet using Newton's laws of motion. Then, in September 1846, guided by Le Verrier's calculations, Johann Gottfried Galle and Heinrich d'Arrest of the Berlin Observatory spotted the elusive planet. It was discovered within 1° of where Le Verrier had predicted it would be. The planet was named Neptune after the Roman god of the sea.

*Mantle of ice, methane and ammonia*

*Rocky silicate core*

## How far away is Neptune ?

Neptune orbits the Sun at a distance of 4,500 million kilometres. It is thirty times further from the Sun than Earth. For this reason, Neptune is extremely cold. The temperature at Neptune's equator is about –230°C.

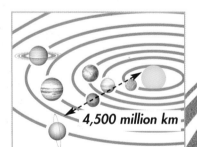

4,500 million km

### FACT BYTES

Neptune has three main rings, which vary in thickness. This was confirmed by the Voyager 2 space probe.

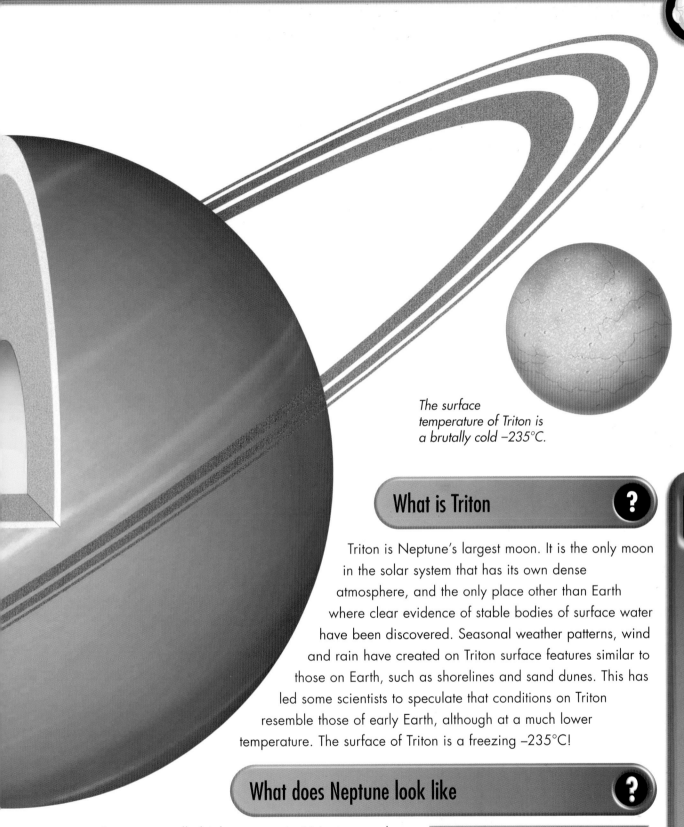

The surface temperature of Triton is a brutally cold −235°C.

## What is Triton ?

Triton is Neptune's largest moon. It is the only moon in the solar system that has its own dense atmosphere, and the only place other than Earth where clear evidence of stable bodies of surface water have been discovered. Seasonal weather patterns, wind and rain have created on Triton surface features similar to those on Earth, such as shorelines and sand dunes. This has led some scientists to speculate that conditions on Triton resemble those of early Earth, although at a much lower temperature. The surface of Triton is a freezing −235°C!

## What does Neptune look like ?

Sometimes called 'planetary twins' Neptune and Uranus are almost identical in many ways, being about 50,000 km in diameter and coloured blue-green. Neptune rotates on its axis every sixteen hours, and Uranus, seventeen.

*Neptune (left) looks similar to Uranus (right).*

# PLUTO

Formerly the smallest planet in the solar system, Pluto was reclassified as a 'dwarf planet' after the International Astronomical Union changed the meaning of the term 'planet' in 2006. This remote ball of ice has three known moons. Charon, Pluto's closest moon, is about half the size of Pluto itself.

*Crust*

*Core of rock and ice*

*Icy mantle*

## Who discovered Pluto, and how did they do it ?

In 1905, Percival Lowell discovered that the force of gravity from some unknown object was affecting the orbits of Uranus and Neptune. In 1915 he predicted the existence of a new planet, but died in 1916 without finding it. Clyde Tombaugh, a young farm worker employed to work at the

Lowell Observatory in Arizona, used the predictions made by Lowell to find Pluto, which he did in 1930. Named after the god of the underworld, Pluto also honours Percival Lowell, whose initials are the first two letters of Pluto.

*Clyde Tombaugh.*

## Is Pluto a real planet ?

In 2006, the International Astronomical Union decided that Pluto should be reclassified as a 'dwarf planet'. The decision was made by astronomers who argued that Pluto shared its orbit with too many asteroids to be considered an independent planet. After the reclassification, Pluto was added to the list of minor planets and given the number '134340'. There are two other known dwarf planets in our solar system. They are called Eris and Ceres.

*An artist's impression of Pluto's surface.*

## FACT BYTES

Astronomers of Pluto is ab

Pluto is tiny –

## How far is Pluto from the Sun

Pluto's orbit is different from those of the planets. While the planets have a circular orbit, Pluto's orbit is eccentric, which means that at certain points of its orbit it is closer to the Sun than at other times (Pluto's orbit takes it to within 4.34 billion km of the Sun and as far away as 7.4 billion km). This means that Pluto is sometimes closer to the Sun than Neptune. The last time this happened was between 1979 and 1999.

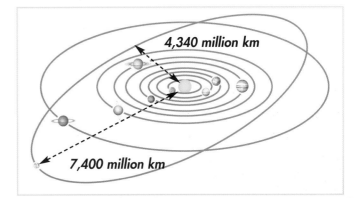

*4,340 million km*

*7,400 million km*

## What is Charon ?

**PLUTO**

Pluto has three known moons. They are called Hydra, Nix and Charon. Discovered in 1978, Charon is Pluto's largest and nearest moon. Charon was discovered in 1978, when astronomer James Flagstaff noticed that images of Pluto were slightly elongated on photographs he had taken. Pluto and Charon are tidally locked to each other. This means that they continuously face each other as they travel around the Sun.

If you were standing on Pluto's near side, Charon would seem to hover in the sky without moving.

t the surface temperature

rds the size of our Moon!

*Charon is half the size of Pluto. The planet and its moon are very close to each other – only 19,600 km apart.*

# THE STARS

When you look up into the night sky and see it filled with stars, just think that each one could be like our own Sun, capable of supporting life and its own solar system. Of all different ages and sizes, stars continue to be born, and to die. We tend to view them in groups called constellations, which help us to make sense of the sheer size and distance of stars themselves.

## How far away are the stars ❓

The closest star, apart from the Sun, is just over four light years away and the dimmest stars we can see without a telescope are thousands of light years away. We see nearby stars as they looked several years ago and faraway stars as they looked thousands of years ago.

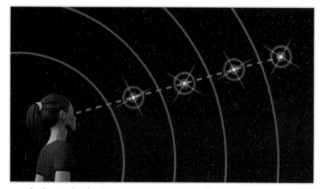

*With the naked eye, we can see stars four light years away.*

## Why are stars different colours ❓

If you look carefully at the stars with binoculars or a telescope, you will see that they range in colour from red to yellow to blue. The different colours are caused by temperature. Measured in Kelvins (K), red stars have surface temperatures that range between 2500–3500$^K$. Yellow stars are about 5500$^K$ and blue stars range from 10,000 to 50,000$^K$.

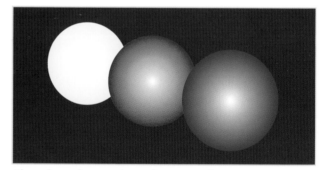

*The colour of a star depends on its surface temperature.*

## What are the 'hemispheres' ❓

Earth is split around the middle by an imaginary line called the equator. Whether you are situated above or below it determines whether you're in the northern or southern hemisphere. The stars you can see depend on where you are on Earth. The most easily recognisable star in the northern hemisphere is the Pole Star (Polaris). The southern hemisphere's most famous star is the Dog Star (Sirius).

*Spot some famous star constellations in the northern hemisphere: 1) Pegasus, 2) Cygnus, 3) Cassiopeia, 4) Bootes, 5) Ursa Major, 6) Leo, 7) top of Orion.*

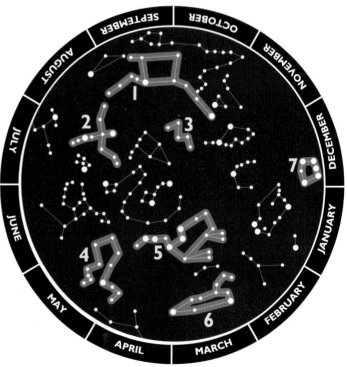

*In the southern hemisphere, you can see: 1) bottom of Orion,
2) Canis Major, 3) Phoenix, 4) Southern Cross, 5) Pavo, 6) Scorpius.*

## What is a constellation ?

A constellation is simply a set of stars that have been put into a group that forms a recognised pattern, and given a name. There are 88 groups of stars that can be called constellations. Many of them were named by the ancient Greeks after animals and people from myths and legends.

### FACT BYTES

The Sun you felt on your skin today was produced one million years ago! It takes an immense amount of time for the rays to work their way to the solar surface.

## What is a 'nova' ?

A 'nova' is a sudden brightening of a star. A nova may occur in a stellar system that has two stars – a white dwarf (sleeping star) and another star. If these two stars are close enough to each other, material from the star can be pulled off its surface and onto the white dwarf. Occasionally, the temperature of this new material on the surface of the white dwarf may become hot enough to reignite the sleeping star. This causes the white dwarf to suddenly become very bright – a nova!

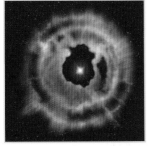

*A nova is 100,000 brighter.*

*A star reaches the end of its life.*

## How long do stars last ?

It all depends how much hydrogen the star started off with. Heavy stars tend to burn brightly but die out quickly. Don't worry! Our Sun has billions of years of useful life left before it runs out of hydrogen. It is around half-way through its 'life' as a star.

*Our star will burn for much longer before running out!*

**THE STARS**

25

# GALAXIES

**Vast, rotating masses of stars, dust and gas, galaxies exist in huge numbers and are held together by gravity. Our solar system forms part of the galaxy known as the Milky Way, which consists of maybe 100 to 200 billion other stars and measures around 100,000 light years across!**

## What is the Milky Way ?

Astronomers estimate that our galaxy, the Milky Way, is one of billions of other galaxies in the universe. The Milky Way contains about 200 billion stars, our Sun being one of them. It is 100,000 light years across. Our solar system is tiny in comparison to the size of the Milky Way, which can be seen clearly from Earth with a telescope. The great bulge in the centre of our galaxy is known as the nucleus, and contains older stars.

Before telescopes, the Milky Way was viewed as a blurred, white streak across the sky. The ancient Greeks and the Romans named it 'a river of milk' and a 'road of milk', leading to its name today.

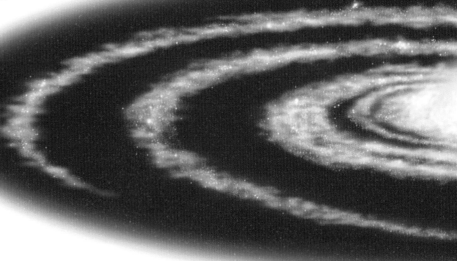

## Where is our solar system located inside our galaxy ?

Our solar system is nearer to the edge than the middle of our galaxy, the Milky Way. When we look into the night sky and see the Milky Way we are seeing through the edge of our galaxy. If you look towards the southern constellations of Sagittarius, you will be looking towards the central bulge and if you look towards constellations like the W-shaped Cassiopeia you will be facing the outer edge.

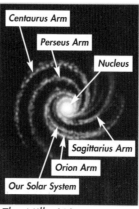

Centaurus Arm
Perseus Arm
Nucleus
Sagittarius Arm
Orion Arm
Our Solar System

*The Milky Way.*

*Our galaxy edge-on.*

FACT B

Astrono
our gala
billion y

Through
are mor
estimate
universe

## What is Andromeda

The Andromeda galaxy, also known as Messier 31 (or M31), is only two million light years away and, from dark country sites, can be seen as a faint smudge of light. In the southern hemisphere, the large and small Magellanic clouds can be seen too. They are small companion galaxies orbiting our own galaxy.

## How many galaxies are there

Billions! Astronomers can see countless galaxies as they look further back in space and time with huge telescopes and with the Hubble Space Telescope.

*This image from the Hubble Space Telescope shows galaxies outside our own.*

*An example of a spiral galaxy.*

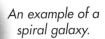

## What shapes are galaxies

Galaxies can be split into different classes, depending on their shape. Spirals, shaped like pinwheels, look like our own galaxy, the Milky Way. Irregular galaxies have no definite shape at all. Elliptical galaxies range in shape from spheres to oval. They are more likely to be the oldest type as, running out of fresh gas, they cannot create many new stars and form a fixed shape. Irregular and spiral galaxies are still growing and their shapes will change as new stars are born.

k that it takes 225 million years for ate. Since it formed, some eleven , it has rotated about fifty times.

unts, astronomers believe that there 00 billion stars in our galaxy and be 80 to 120 billion galaxies in the y can see.

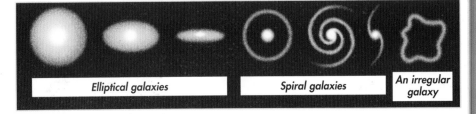

*Elliptical galaxies*     *Spiral galaxies*     *An irregular galaxy*

# BLACK HOLES

Black holes sound like they could be something out of a science fiction story – objects so dense that nothing in the universe can escape from their gravitational pull. However, astronomers have been steadily building up evidence that black holes are not only real, but actually quite common in the universe.

## What is a black hole

Black holes are regions of space where gravity is so strong it gobbles up everything that comes near it – stars, planets, gases and even light! That is why the hole is 'black'. Black holes are invisible, but we know that they exist because we can see the stuff that is being sucked in to them!

The edge of a black hole is known as the 'event horizon' – the point of no return. Even if something could get inside a black hole, there would be no way that it could 'get back' as it would disappear completely, and forever! As something is pulled inside, it is first torn apart by immense gravitational force and then it forms a flat rotating disc that spirals into the hole.

## How do we know they exist

Black holes can be detected only by their effects on the space surrounding them. As material gets closer and closer to a black hole it speeds up and bits start to smash together. This creates heat which scientists are able to detect. If the black hole is really large and has lots of debris in its disc, then it can reveal itself as one of the brightest objects in the universe – a quasar.

## How does a black hole form ?

The most likely cause of a black hole, or so astronomers think, is a massive star coming to the end of its life. The star collapses, because the fuel has run out, and the energy provided by the nuclear reactions can no longer support the star's weight. When the star collapses it becomes very dense and its gravitational pull increases. If the escape velocity exceeds the speed of light, the star is swallowed by its own gravity and only the gravitational pull remains.

The star collapses after all of its 'fuel' runs out.

The star becomes very dense.

The star is swallowed by its own gravity.

## FACT BYTES

A feather would weigh several billion tonnes in a black hole!

If an astronaut 'fell' into a black hole, he or she would be stretched like a piece of spaghetti by the huge gravitational pull.

A su
coul
gala

## What are wormholes ?

There is a theory that a black hole can form a tunnel through space called a wormhole. It is thought that if you entered a wormhole, you would travel through space and arrive in another universe. Although mathematically possible, wormholes would be extremely unstable and probably do not exist.

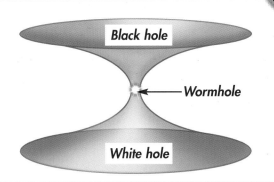

Black hole

Wormhole

White hole

Event horizon

Supermassive black hole

Spiralling hot gases

...ive black hole
...he centre of our

## What is a supermassive black hole ?

Supermassive black holes are perhaps the most strange, destructive and terrifying objects in the universe! Billions of times bigger than our Sun, these powerful monsters may lurk at the centre of every galaxy – the Milky Way included. Some scientists believe that these forces of destruction trigger the birth of galaxies and therefore are at the heart of the creation of stars, planets and all life.

# CELESTIAL BODIES

Along with the planets, stars and galaxies, there are comets, meteors and asteroids whizzing around the Sun, producing amazing shows of lights. Members of NASA have devised a mechanism called the Torino Scale to assess the damage celestial bodies could do if they hit Earth. Fortunately, any serious collisions with Earth are incredibly rare!

## What is a comet ?

A typical comet is a chunk of icy and rocky material that releases gas and dust. If this icy chunk gets close to the Sun, it heats up and the icy material evaporates, creating the comet's coma, the surrounding clouds and atmosphere and its tail. Comets can be between 1 km and 50 km in diameter, whereas the comet's tail can be millions of kilometres long even though the comet itself is small.

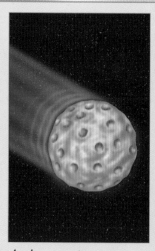 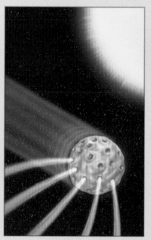

*An icy comet...*     *...is heated by the Sun.*

## What is a meteor? Is it the same sort of thing ?

A meteor is a tiny particle which enters Earth's atmosphere from space. Typically, it might only be the size of a grain of sand but, as it heats up and glows, it looks like a star shooting across the sky. Most meteors burn up before reaching Earth. Occasionally, however, a meteor is too big to burn up before reaching Earth's surface. The meteors that reach Earth are called meteorites, and vary in size and weight. Most are very small, but the largest found was about 60 tonnes! At certain times of the year there are meteor showers. The meteors vapourise due to air friction, so the sky is filled with a shower of sparks!

*A 'shooting star'.*

## How many are out there ?

The LINEAR and NEAT telescopes in the USA have discovered hundreds of thousands of tiny asteroids, mainly between Mars and Jupiter. Astronomers also know of over 1,000 comets, although most are too faint to be seen without a big telescope. The possibility of an asteroid hitting Earth is measured on NASA's Torino Scale. However, astronomers have calculated that the chance of a collision with Earth large enough to cause major damage averages out at once every 300,000 years!

## FACT BYTES

Comets' tails don't point to the direction they're travelling, but are pushed away from the Sun by solar winds.

There is some evidence that William the Conqueror saw Halley's comet in 1066.

## Can I see a comet ?

Comets can be seen from Earth when they pass close to the Sun, as the sunlight reflects off the gas and the dust. Every few years a comet becomes visible to the naked eye, and with binoculars, or a small telescope, you can see comets every year.

*Some comets are visible to the naked eye.*

## What is the difference between an asteroid and a comet ?

The main difference between asteroids and comets is what they're made of. While comets are made up of dust, ice and rocky material, asteroids are formed from rocky material and some metals. This means that asteroids don't have a tail, as no ice evaporates from them. Asteroids orbit the Sun, mainly between the planets Mars and Jupiter. They range in size from 1–200 km across. The four largest asteroids known to astronomers are named Ceres, Pallas, Juno and Vesta.

*Heat creates the comet's impressive tail which can be millions of kilometres long.*

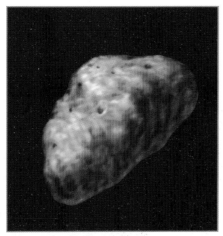

*Asteroids reach 200 km across.*

*The bright spot is called the nucleus.*

# EARLY ROCKETS

The only vehicles powerful enough to carry people and equipment into space, rockets push themselves upwards and forwards using thrust. Without the rocket, we'd know very little about the things you are reading about in this book. We might be able to see certain planets, and our Moon, but we'd never be able to visit them.

## Who invented the rocket ?

The first rockets may have been invented as early as the tenth century, by the Chinese, but they were little more than flying 'fire-arrows' filled with flammable material. By the thirteenth century, however, primitive fireworks and rockets filled with gunpowder were in regular use. In the early 1800s, Colonel William Congreve, a military man based at Woolwich Arsenal, developed a range of rocket missiles which could be launched from special ships in battle.

Congreve rockets could be fired about 2,700 metres.

*The first liquid fuel rocket.*

*Congreve rockets were built on long poles to make them easy to carry into battle.*

## What was a liquid fuel rocket ?

The American Robert Goddard launched the first liquid fuel rocket on 16th March, 1926. It used liquid oxygen and petrol as the propellant. The rocket was over 3 m long and reached a height of just over 12 m and a speed of over 100 km/h. By 1935 his best rocket was nearly 5 m long and could climb to a height of over 2 km at a speed of 1,000 km/h.

*Dr Robert Goddard with an early liquid fuel rocket.*

## Who was the first man to design a space rocket

The Russian Konstantin Tsiolkovsky (1857–1935) designed the first space rockets, although he never actually built any. He was a Russian mathematician and physicist who realised that liquid oxygen and liquid hydrogen would provide the best rocket fuel. His theory, the 'Tsiolkovsky Formula', analysed the relationships between rocket speed and gas pressure. It was not until the mid twentieth century that the first satellite was launched by the Russians.

*Konstantin Tsiolkovsky.*

*The V2 rocket was an impressive development and stood over 15 m tall. It was used to attack London during the Second World War.*

## Who was Wernher von Braun

Wernher von Braun was one of the most important pioneers of rocket development. He was employed under the Nazi regime to build V2 rockets and later transferred to NASA to help develop the Saturn rockets. He was the chief architect of the Saturn V launch vehicle, and is ultimately responsible for getting the first people to the Moon. This technology has been used in many lunar landings since.

### FACT BYTES

NASA stands for National Aeronautics and Space Administration.

It was set up in 1958 as a worldwide body for space exploration and discovery.

## Who launched the first satellite into orbit

For over ten years, the Soviet Union and the United States of America were locked in a development battle known as the 'Space Race'. In 1957, the Soviet Union launched the first artificial satellite, Sputnik 1. It weighed 83 kg and orbited Earth every 96 minutes for three months. The satellite helped to develop our understanding of Earth's atmosphere. The successful launch shocked and amazed the world.

*The Sputnik 1 satellite.*

**EARLY ROCKETS**

Once rocket technology had been developed, it was soon realised that if a missile could be sent across the world, rockets could be sent up into space. At the beginning of the 1960s, another race began between the Soviet Union and the United States of America – the goal being to send the first man into space.

## How fast do rockets go

Rockets can travel up to 40,000 km/h. As they re-enter Earth's atmosphere and prepare for touchdown, the speed drops to a few hundred km/h. A parachute is released, and they slow to a safe speed before landing on land or in the water – if all goes to plan!

*Spacecraft landing safely in the ocean with a parachute.*

## What was the first Moon rocket

The first manned spacecraft was made in April 1961 when Yuri Gagarin orbited Earth in spacecraft Vostok 1. The first manned spacecraft to orbit the Moon and come back was Apollo 8 in December 1968. Apollo 11 landed on the Moon's surface on 20 July 1969, commanded by Neil Armstrong.

## Why are rockets so huge

At the beginning of the race to send a rocket to the Moon, there was no single rocket powerful enough to force through Earth's gravity. The answer to this problem came in the form of rocket stages – putting smaller rockets into giant multi-stage launch vehicles that would tackle each part of lift-off with different sections containing fuel supplies to aid the engines. After each rocket stage has used up its fuel, the stage is discarded, keeping the rocket as light as possible.

## Who was the first man in space

On the 12th April 1961, Russian Yuri Gagarin became the first man in space, His spacecraft *Vostok 1* orbited Earth for 108 minutes. Less than a month later, NASA launched their first astronaut, Alan Shepard into space, but he did not orbit Earth. In February 1962, NASA launched John Glenn into space, where he orbited Earth three times in five hours, reaching speeds of over 27,000 km/h.

*Yuri Gagarin.*

*Alan Shepard.*

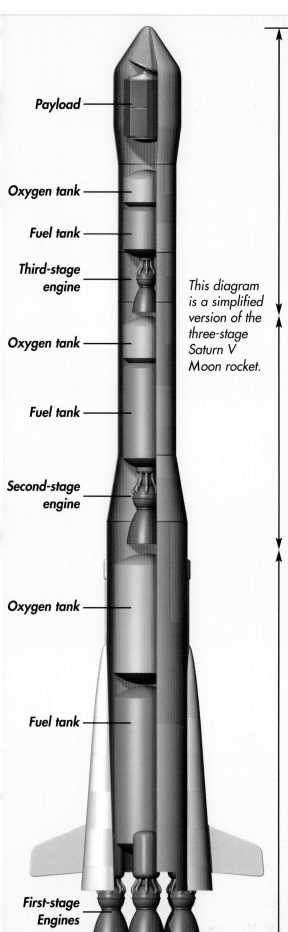

Payload

Oxygen tank

Fuel tank

Third-stage
engine

Oxygen tank

Fuel tank

Second-stage
engine

Oxygen tank

Fuel tank

First-stage
Engines

*This diagram
is a simplified
version of the
three-stage
Saturn V
Moon rocket.*

## Third stage

The third stage is boosted into orbit with a smaller engine, which is discarded with stages one and two once the spacecraft is safely in orbit, or on the way to the Moon.

## Second stage

Liquid oxygen in the oxygen tank mixes with the fuel in the fuel tank of the second-stage engine, pushing the rocket to a higher altitude – around 185 km. Once used, it is discarded.

## First stage

The first-stage rocket contains enough fuel to feed the engines which provide enough lift for the huge weight of the rocket to escape gravity (i.e. – not fall back down again!). Once used, the first one is discarded.

## How large are space rockets ?

The Ariane 5, launched on 21st October, 1998, marked the beginning of a new style of heavyweight rocket. Its total height (including all stages) was 59 m, with a diameter of about 6 m. The

*The Ariane 5 rocket.*

Saturn V rocket that launched the Apollo spacecraft weighed over 3,000 tonnes. Nearly all of that weight was fuel!

*Most of this rocket contains fuel for the mission.*

# INSIDE A SPACECRAFT

Living in space may seem like fun. After all, there's no gravity to hold you down so your body floats. However, simple things we take for granted here on Earth, like taking a shower or going to the toilet, are a mission of their own inside a spacecraft. All astronauts must go through lots of preparation before they are considered ready for a journey that could last for months.

*The Shuttle is divided into three sections: the flight deck, living quarters, and lower deck. Everything, including the astronauts when they go to bed, must be strapped down!*

## How does space travel affect astronauts ❓

The body's weightlessness in space means that bone and muscle can easily waste away as there is little work for the muscle to do when the body weighs so little. Without gravity the spine starts to relax, and astronauts can easily be 5 cm taller at the end of a mission. This height increase quickly goes away again after a few days back on Earth. To keep fit, the astronauts eat a special diet and exercise regularly while they are weightless. More than two-thirds of astronauts suffer from motion sickness, although most recover after a few days in space.

Controls for pay[l]

Observation window

Pilot's seat

Exercise cham[ber]

Bunk beds

*Astronauts can become taller in space as lack of gravity causes the spine to relax.*

## Why are spacesuits essential ❓

The atmosphere in space is very different to that on Earth, so a spacesuit provides astronauts with air to breathe when they go for a walk outside the spacecraft. There is also no air pressure in space, so even if an astronaut could hold his breath he could not go into space as his lungs would burst from the pressure inside his body. Spacesuits provide protection from the extreme temperatures in space, too. Cold water was pumped around the suits used by the astronauts travelling to the Moon to keep them cool. The helmet on a spacesuit provides a protective dark visor to reduce the Sun's intense glare in space.

## How do astronauts take a shower ❓

Water is a very precious resource in space, so astronauts can go for days without a shower, just sponging themselves with damp cloths. On some spacecraft, a special 'shower' unit is fitted. The astronaut gets into the cylinder, shuts the door and then soaps up with a wet pad – lack of gravity means that the water sticks to the body, so it has to be rubbed off. Any soapy mess is sucked up using a special attachment!

*A space shower is very different than on Earth!*

*Conmmander's seat*

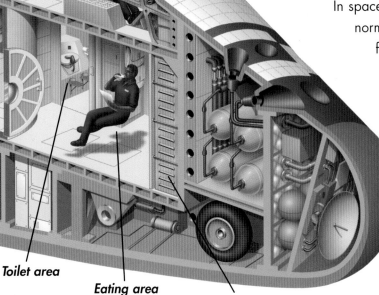

*Toilet area*

*Eating area*

*Ladder to flight deck*

## How do astronauts eat food in space ❓

In space, everything is weightless, which makes eating a normal meal impossible. All the food and the knives, forks and plates would just float around! Liquids would float away from cups too. To combat these problems, astronauts have special packs of food containing liquidised food which they can suck through a straw. Some of the meals are dehydrated so water is added to them through a straw, and then sucked up. Food like fruit can be eaten in its natural form.

*Space food must be freeze-dried.*

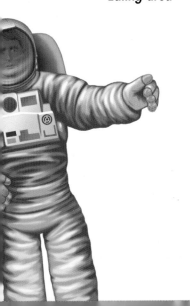

### FACT BYTES

There are no definite explanations as to why food tastes different in space. Some astronauts pack plenty of their favourite food, only to find they can't stand it after lift-off!

Astronauts often suffer from 'stuffy head' – they feel 'blocked up' around the upper half of the body because their blood flows in an upward direction!

Food must be freeze-dried to remove water to make it as light as possible. Bizarrely, the nutritional value remains nearly the same!

*Grub's up!*

**INSIDE A SPACECRAFT**

# MOON LANDING MISSIONS

**The world watched with bated breath as NASA sent men to the Moon in 1969. From 1969 to 1972, six missions and twelve astronauts landed on the Moon, but there have been no more manned landings since. Several nations, including China and India, have plans to send man back to the Moon within decades.**

## Who were the first people to land ?

The first men to set foot on the Moon's surface were Neil Armstrong and Edwin 'Buzz' Aldrin on 20th July, 1969. It took them around four days to get there. They spent two and a half hours collecting soil samples and taking photographs. While on the Moon, they spoke to US President Richard Nixon in the White House and planted a US flag. When Armstrong stepped on to the Moon, he uttered the phrase 'One small step for man, one giant leap for mankind'.

*The image beamed to millions on TV sets.*

## FACT BYTES

An orange glass-like substance has been found on the Moon's surface, suggesting that there was once some volcanic activity.

The Moon does not have a 'weather' system, so its rocks are not exposed to wind or water. Therefore, Buzz Aldrin's footprints are as fresh as when he made them!

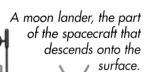
*A moon lander, the part of the spacecraft that descends onto the surface.*

## Will man return to the Moon in the future

NASA's plans to return men to the Moon received a setback in 2010 when President Obama cancelled the 'Constellation Program'. However, Russia, Europe, China, Japan and India have all stated their aims for manned flights and finally moon bases. The near future of Moon exploration may be robotic, rather than human.

## What were the Apollo landings ?

Between 1969 and 1972, Apollo spacecraft landed on the Moon six times. Each mission lasted around twelve days and astronauts visited different places each time. Astronomers gave these spots different names, like the 'Sea of Tranquility' (a smooth area of ancient lava) and 'Hadley Rille' – a V-shaped gorge, meandering amongst large mountains. The astronauts on Apollo 15 travelled 25 km in a Land-Roving Vehicle (LRV), an electrically powered four-wheel drive. An attempt by Apollo 13 failed to land as there was an onboard explosion, but the spacecraft did manage to return to Earth safely.

## Why were the landings so important

A lot was learnt from the manned missions to the Moon – enough information was gathered for scientists to work on for decades! Tonnes of lunar rock was brought back to Earth and hundreds of photographs were taken. During the missions, astronauts left experiments on the surface of the Moon, which sent data back to Earth for many years. Earth's magnetism was measured, along with the distance between Earth and the Moon. The missions proved that human beings could live and work in space without suffering ill effects.

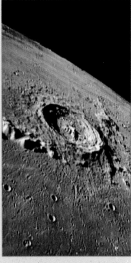
*Lunar craters.*

*Earth and the Moon.*

# RETURN TO EARTH

Once astronauts had gathered all the evidence they needed, taking samples from a landing or images from space, they had to return to Earth. This needed very careful planning to ensure that their craft, the Space Shuttle, descended safely as it pushed through Earth's atmosphere. The Space Shuttle no longer operates, but this is how it worked.

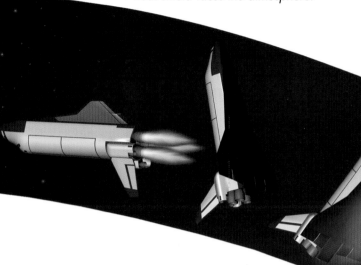

*Retro-rockets fire to slow the Shuttle down and the spacecraft turns so the heat shield faces the atmosphere.*

## How does re-entry happen ?

Returning to Earth requires a great deal of skill and planning. The trick is to enter Earth's atmosphere at just the right angle to slow the spacecraft down safely, without using up huge amounts of fuel. The pilot receives instructions from 'space station control' on Earth to help them navigate. Earth's atmosphere also acts as a drag, slowing down the shuttle.

## Why is re-entry difficult ?

If the craft enters at too shallow an angle it will bounce off the atmosphere. If it enters at too steep an angle it will burn up and hit the ground at great speed. By entering the atmosphere at the correct angle, the spacecraft will be able to reduce the heat and resistance generated, eventually landing safely.

*A deck in a spacecraft.*

*A space station's controls.*

*As the Shuttle approaches, it becomes a huge glider, landing with no engines at over 320 km/h.*

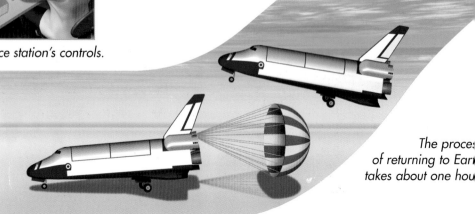

*As the Shuttle has no reverse thrust jet engines, a parachute and wheel brakes finally bring it to a stop.*

*The proces of returning to Ear takes about one hou*

## What happened to the Space Shuttle Columbia ?

*The Shuttle usually starts to re-enter the atmosphere on the dark side of the planet.*

On 1st February, 2003 the Space Shuttle *Columbia* burned up on re-entry, killing all seven astronauts. A large chunk of insulation foam, which fell off the fuel tank at lift-off, damaged the Shuttle's heat-resistant tiles, causing the spacecraft to overheat and break up on re-entry. In 1986, seven astronauts were killed when the Shuttle *Challenger* developed a fault with its boosters.

*The Space Shuttle* Columbia *blasts off.*

*Below 1,600 km/h, the Shuttle starts to land like a normal aircraft, weaving in S-shaped curves to further reduce speed.*

*The Shuttle enters the densest parts of the atmosphere at about 12,000 m above Earth.*

### FACT BYTES

Some Shuttles touch down onto a runway, in a similar way to a plane. They have a lifting body design and swept-back wings. When an orbiter 'touches down' this way, the descent rate is SEVEN times steeper than that of an airliner!

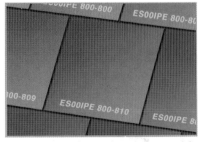

*The ceramic heat tiles are reusable but take a real bashing when they re-enter the atmosphere.*

## What are heat-resistant tiles ?

A Space Shuttle is covered with 20,000 tiles that can withstand up to four times more heat than they encounter upon re-entry. The tiles are made of a material that can be hot on one side but cool on the other. NASA Space Shuttles are designed to be reusable. When they re-enter Earth's atmosphere many of the tiles are damaged and need to be replaced. It's easier to replace small tiles than one huge heat shield.

**RETURN TO EARTH**

# SATELLITES

A satellite is any object that orbits or revolves around another. In addition to the Moon (a natural satellite), thousands of man-made satellites also orbit Earth. They are used for many different purposes, including satellite television, phone calls, radio transmissions, Internet connections, weather forecasting, scientific research and surveillance.

*'Space junk' – de[...] from broken up sate[...]*

*Sol[...]*

## How high are the satellites ?

Many scientific satellites are only 300–400 km above Earth and orbit in under two hours. As these satellites are relatively close to Earth, they require little fuel and are cheap to launch. Major communications satellites are put at a huge distance of 36,000 km from Earth. At this distance, an orbit takes exactly one day to complete.

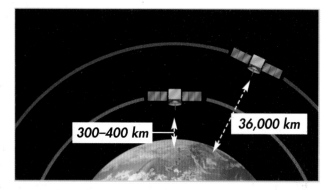

*300–400 km*    *36,000 km*

## How many man-made satellites are out there ?

Since the late 1950s, thousands of satellites have been launched. Many of the early satellites have fallen back to Earth and burned up in the atmosphere. There are also thousands of items of 'space-junk', such as rocket boosters and fuel tanks that have not burned up in orbit. Today, there are about 3,000 useful satellites and 6,000 pieces of 'space junk' orbiting Earth.

## What does a satellite do ?

The working satellites orbiting Earth are of various types. There are telephone, TV and radio communications satellites, military spy satellites, weather satellites and satellites studying the Sun and distant objects in the universe. There is also the Hubble Space Telescope which is one of the largest objects orbiting Earth. The biggest object is the *International Space Station*.

*We use satellites to communicate.*

*Some are used by the military.*

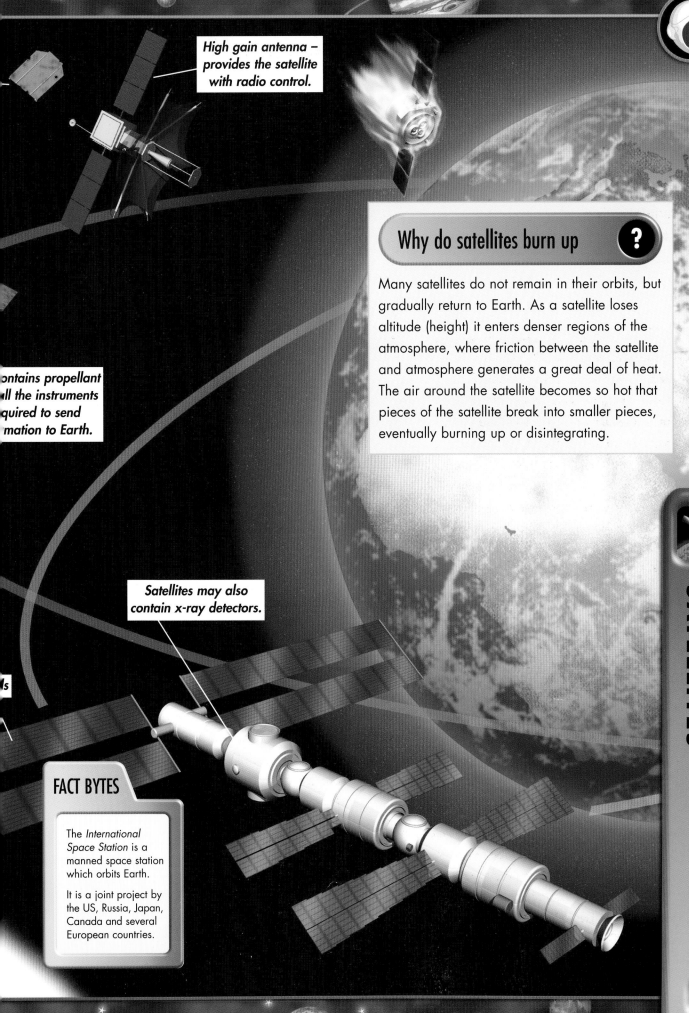

High gain antenna – provides the satellite with radio control.

ontains propellant
ll the instruments
quired to send
mation to Earth.

## Why do satellites burn up ?

Many satellites do not remain in their orbits, but gradually return to Earth. As a satellite loses altitude (height) it enters denser regions of the atmosphere, where friction between the satellite and atmosphere generates a great deal of heat. The air around the satellite becomes so hot that pieces of the satellite break into smaller pieces, eventually burning up or disintegrating.

Satellites may also contain x-ray detectors.

### FACT BYTES

The *International Space Station* is a manned space station which orbits Earth.

It is a joint project by the US, Russia, Japan, Canada and several European countries.

# FUTURE MISSIONS

**So what does the future of space travel hold? In the last century, humans have achieved things astronomers such as William Herschel could only dream of, with satellite images and Moon missions. If we are ever to send manned missions to the distant planets of our solar system and beyond, some mighty challenges need to be overcome and major new technologies developed.**

## Should we use humans or robots ?

Although sending human beings into space was a great achievement, small robotic explorers appear to be the most efficient way of exploring space. The advances in computing power in recent years mean that very powerful and lightweight robot explorers can land on planets like Mars and explore the surface. Human beings are heavy and need lots of food, water and oxygen wherever they go. The biggest advantage to using machines is that if robot explorers get destroyed it is just an expensive accident, but human beings cannot be replaced.

A Mars Exploration Rover.

## Will humans ever visit Mars ?

1 year

1 year

For decades, governments and space agencies have considered sending manned missions to Mars. In 2007, NASA hinted that they may be able to launch a human mission to Mars by 2037. The European Space Agency has the long-term vision of sending a human mission to Mars by 2030. Some scientists have criticised those plans, arguing that manned missions to Mars would be too expensive and that funding would be better spent developing space technology such as robots.

## How can we travel to distant planets more quickly ?

One of the most likely methods of powering spacecrafts to distant planets would be to use nuclear power. Nuclear rockets are more powerful than existing chemically-fired launchers, and rockets run by nuclear fission are fuel efficient and light. They could reach Saturn in three years instead of seven. Missions would become easier, as the need to carry food, fuel and oxygen would be reduced. In 2003, NASA established Project Prometheus, a project that develops nuclear-powered systems for long distance missions. However, in 2005 the project faced an uncertain future and eventually it was cancelled.

### FACT BYTES

Over 3 million people had their names burned onto an electronic disk attached to one of the Exploration Rovers that was sent to Mars.

## Where will we go next ?

During the past forty years, there have been huge changes and developments in space flight. Most astronomers would like to think that at some point mankind will spread out into the solar system and explore other galaxies. However, as there are no really fast spaceships, it would take years even to get to the closest planets in our solar system. Rockets are propelled by controlled explosions and not much has changed in the last 40 years. To travel further into space, new ways of powering spacecraft need to be developed.

*The next generation of space exploration needs faster spaceships.*

# GLOSSARY

**Astronaut**
A person trained for travelling in space.

**Astronomer**
Those who study stars, planets and the universe.

**Astrophysics**
The branch of astronomy that is concerned with the physical side of stars and planets.

**Atmosphere**
The layer of gas surrounding Earth or other planets.

**Big bang**
A cataclysmic explosion that scientists believe created time and space.

**Big crunch**
What might happen if the universe stops expanding and collapses on itself.

**Billion**
A thousand million (1,000,000,000).

**Black hole**
A region of space caused by the collapse of a star, so dense that neither matter or radiation can escape.

**Cassiopeia**
An easily-spotted W-shaped constellation near the Pole Star.

**Comet**
Pieces of ice and dust which orbit the Sun.

**Constellation**
Any of the 88 groups of stars as seen from Earth, named by the Greeks after mythological people, objects or animals.

**Corona**
The very hot outer layer of the Sun's atmosphere.

**Ellipse**
A shape like a flattened circle.

**Equator**
The name for the imaginary band around the middle of Earth that splits it into two hemispheres, the north and the south.

**Evening Star**
Another common name for Venus.

**Fission**
The splitting of the centres of heavy atoms into lighter ones.

**Fusion**
The combining of lighter elements into heavier ones.

**Galaxy**
A collection of billions of stars held together by gravitational attraction.

**Great Red Spot**
A long-lived feature on Jupiter's surface, south of its equator, which has survived for hundreds of years.

**Hemispheres**
The two halves of the globe, as divided by an imaginary line around the middle called the equator.

**Hydrosphere**
The water on, or around, the surface of a planet.

**International Space Station**
A permanently manned satellite constructed between 1998 and 2001 for space research.

**Kelvin**
A temperature scale used by astronomers, in which the lowest possible temperature is called 'absolute zero'.

**Lunar-Roving Vehicle**
An electronically powered four-wheel drive vehicle that can explore planets' surface.

**Light year**
The distance that light travels in one year. It is equal to just under 10 trillion kilometres!

**LINEAR**
Also NEAT – Telescopes which discover asteroids and comets.

**Lunar eclipse**
When Earth passes between the Sun and the Moon.

**Magnetosphere**
A magnetic field around the Sun and certain planets.

**Magnitude scale**
The scale on which objects are measured for their brightness.

**Mariner**
A series of American space probes which visited Mercury, Venus and Mars.

**Messier**
A catalogue named after an eighteenth century astronomer which identifies galaxies and nebulae etc. by their number i.e. M31 (Andromeda Galaxy).

**Meteor**
A very small iron or rocky particle that has entered Earth's atmosphere. Also called a shooting star.

**Milky Way**
A spiral galaxy containing billions of stars, our solar system and Earth.

**Miranda**
One of Uranus' largest moons, with a unique surface.

**NASA**
The National Aeronautics and Space Administration is an agency of the United States government responsible for the nation's public space programme.

**Nova**
When a star undergoes an eruption and suddenly becomes much brighter for a short period.

**Observatory**
A building specially designed to look at astrological objects.

**Olympus Mons**
A massive volcano on the surface of Mars.

**Orbit**
The regularly repeated path of a moon, spacecraft etc. around a star or planet.

**Photosphere**
The area of the Sun that we look at, face-on.

**Radiative zone**
The heat from the Sun's core is passed through this zone, and the energy transfer begins. It then reaches the less dense area of the convective zone where it rises and starts to reach the atmosphere.

**Rings**
Any of the thin, circular bands made from small components that orbit something larger i.e. Saturn.

**Satellite**
A satellite is an object that rotates around or orbits another object. They can be man-made like the communications satellites that orbit Earth; or natural like the Moon that orbits Earth.

**Sea of Tranquility**
A smooth area of ancient lava on the surface of the Moon – made famous by the Apollo 11 landing.

**Solar eclipse**
When the Moon comes between the Sun and Earth.

**Solar flare**
A sudden brightening near a sunspot.

**Solar System**
The system containing the Sun and other bodies in its gravitational field, including the Moon and eight known planets.

**Sunspot**
A dark blemish on the solar surface that is caused by the Sun's magnetic field.

**Sunspot cycle**
The eleven-year cycle that sees the rise and fall in the number of sunspots.

**Supernova**
When a star runs out of fuel, it becomes unstable and appears 100 million times brighter for a few days before 'dying'.

**White dwarf**
A small, very dense star that has come to the end of its life.

GLOSSARY

# SPACE INDEX

Key: Top – t; middle – m; bottom – b; left – l; right – r

Front and back cover: Stephen Sweet, Photodisc and Corel.

**2:** (bl) NASA. **5:** (tr) Topham Picturepoint. **22:** Science Photo Library. **32:** (t, bl) NASA. **33:** (t, br) NASA. **34:** NASA. **35:** (tr) 2002 ESA - ARIANESPACE/ Photo Service Otique CSG. **37:** (tr, br) NASA. 38: (t) Corel. **39:** (bm) NASA. **41:** (tr) NASA. **44:** (ml) NASA. **48:** NASA.

Illustrations by Stephen Sweet/SGA.